FANTASY FOOTBALL UNLEASHED

55 Tips, Tricks, & Ways to Win at Fantasy Football

The Fantasy Footballers Podcast

Cover design by: Andrew Schneider
Edited by: Kyle Borgognoni, Emily Holloway
Library of Congress Control Number: 2018675309
Printed in the United States of America

This book is dedicated to our wives Tiffany, Amber, and Bri.

Thank you for letting the three of us run after
a silly thing like fantasy football.

CONTENTS

INTRODUCTION

A Holistic Approach To Fantasy Football

When we started The Fantasy Footballers Podcast many years ago, we approached the fantasy football world through a slightly different lens than those that came before.

Yes, fantasy football is a world of stats and analytics. They're core to the fantasy football universe and should always be central to what we do in projecting players and looking at potential outcomes. They are fundamental in every way!

However, fantasy football is about a lot *more* than stats and analytics. Fantasy football is also about decision making. Not simply about players, but about your individual league. It's about your individual week, your individual opponent, and how to make specific decisions about each particular scenario within your individual league context. It's about trading and transactions. It's about finding a few advantages each and every week that give you the best opportunity to win. It's about playing percentages. And it's about fun.

We all play fantasy football because it represents the best in sports -- competition, connection, and adding something to your week that amplifies what you watch on Sundays. It's about the people within your league and the frivolous fun that a fantasy league can provide. It's about taunting one another, mocking one another, enduring the occasional defeat, and gloating once you have a few wins of your own.

Over the past several years, we've done thousands of episodes focused on how to win at fantasy football. Our podcast has won more than thirty industry and podcasting awards, and helped tens of thousands of fantasy managers compete and win each and every season. Each year our expertise grades out among the most accurate in the industry -- something we're proud of -- yet fantasy football dominance goes well beyond player accuracy.

This book is a distilled selection of 55 tips, tricks, and ways that you can think differently about fantasy football and come out on top each and every year. We encourage you to subscribe to our year long podcast as you move forward in your journey towards fantasy football championships. These tips and tricks are quick and concise nuggets to be tucked away and used in your future league-winning efforts.

Yes, there is plenty of luck involved in fantasy football. However, you can overcome the odds more often than not by putting yourself in a position to succeed using these tips, tricks, and insights into the world of fantasy football. We hope you enjoy this book and consider sharing it with others who are just beginning their fantasy football journey.

~ Andy Holloway
The Fantasy Footballers

FANTASY PHILOSOPHY 101

"Luck is what happens when preparation meets opportunity." - Seneca

◆ ◆ ◆

1. Find The Right League

Fantasy football is only as fun as the league you find yourself in and the people you play with. It's not enjoyable to participate in a league where three-fourths of the teams are completely checked out. Winning a title against committed members is an entirely better feeling than winning against two or three. Part of finding the right league is not boxing yourself into a league size. If you have eight committed members, then your league should be eight strong. Move forward, make your league fun, and slowly invite others into an experience and a community -- not just another casual work league. Find people you can communicate with. Talking with people outside of draft day is what makes the league great. Better a smaller league with committed players than a larger one where inactivity destroys the league's integrity. If you're not in the right league, find one.

2. You Don't Win Your League At The Draft

If you want to win your championship, this could be the most important tip you read: **You don't win your league at the draft.** You set the foundation for your season. Don't overvalue players you drafted and assume because your team looks good on paper you can simply coast to victory. Jason is notorious for preaching this advice each and every year because neglecting it resulted in his downfall in a league he thought was wrapped up in his early days. The draft is the foundation and the initial push you need to begin a five month journey towards victory and a #FootClanTitle. You need to be ready and willing to adjust your opinions and thoughts about each and every player you drafted. After an offseason of hype, be willing to move forward with confidence after your draft. The Ultimate Draft Kit can help you set the foundation, but it goes beyond draft day.

3. Stay Water

As an extension of the point above, it's important to be pliable and humble about your opinions. If you have a strong opinion on a player, give yourself room to be able to have your stance change. Beyond petty hype, if you plant your flag and post in your league forum about a player, it can be dangerous as you experience what the guys call #TakeLock. Don't declare wins on players too early. Situations change, rosters suddenly change, and injuries can creep in. Stay water, be willing and ready to adjust, repeat. There's no room for pride on the path to a fantasy championship.

4. Reflect & React

Let's start with the basics. Becoming a better fantasy football player is not always about finding the right sleepers or simply devouring as much new information as possible. Even if you won your league title last year, you always need to be looking back. Reflecting upon your presumptions of certain teams and players can give you an edge and help you not repeat the same mistakes every year. It's about using the past season to assess both analytically your choices as well as where there is inherent bias that creeps in. Start with a simple pad and pen and write down the first three to five thoughts you had from last season. Try to remember what worked and what didn't. We all make mistakes, but you should try not to repeat the same mistakes. Small adjustments year to year can fine tune your strategies.

5. Stay Connected

There are so many resources available for the fantasy football manager. These aren't the days of walking out to the curb, picking up a newspaper, and checking the box scores and news columns for our information. Twitter and social media allows access to beat reporters, fantasy analysts, and even players at an intimate level. Staying connected to the most recent news is key to your success. Sometimes all it takes is being the first one to the information to gain an advantage. Subscribing to a podcast and making it part of your daily routine is such an easy way to stay consistent and remain sharp, whether you're working out, commuting to work, or listening while doing chores at home. Engage, watch, read, and react with a variety of sources. Staying connected is an edge you can gain over your opponents. Make a point of connecting to valuable resources.

A LEAGUE OF YOUR OWN

"Creativity is intelligence having fun." - Albert Einstein

◆ ◆ ◆

6. More Than A Game

Traditions are fantasy gold. Around here, we all know what the *"Holloway"* is: it's congratulating your opponent on their victory the MINUTE you get slightly behind; a superstitious joke as a means to pull out the win. Get in your opponents head. Jason is known as basically the worst winner of all time. He's mouthy. He's known for it. And we love it. You may personally enjoy driving down the value of players who reside on the teams of good managers. It's an all out publicity war against their trade value. Make traditions. Build joy. Taunt, gloat, and dance about. This is more than a game; it's an opportunity to lord over your leaguemates all season. Rivalries and traditions are what make any sport (or fantasy sports) great.

7. Listen To Your Leaguemates

4

Scouting your league is vital to success. You can carry a major advantage by going back to a previous year's drafts and look ing to see someone's tendencies. Perhaps a manager in your league loves quarterbacks early or they love following the hype of certain rookie running backs every single year. Perhaps a manager has a hometown bias. Maybe they follow certain fantasy personalities from big media outlets and they are ready to copy and paste someone else's strategy. Look at your league trends. Every league is different because of the personalities and convictions of each individual manager, but there are predictable behaviors available in every league. You might want fantasy analysts to give you the play-by-play, but remember that your own league determines the context for your decisions. It's the second layer of strategy crucial to yearly success.

8. Know Your League, Not Just Your Roster

The way your leaguemates play affects the way you trade, the way you sign players, and the way you have to think about match-ups. Not every piece of information you consume during the off-season and week-to-week in the NFL season is going to apply to your league. Know your league rules and the people in it as they are your weekly opponents. Filtering advice from podcasts, rankings, and articles through your league format is a necessary process for calibration and honing in on what moves to actually make each week. This may include scoring settings, transaction rules, roster sizes, etc. Distill information through the lens of your own league.

9. Water Bets

Whether you play fantasy football for bragging rights or something a little greener, there is always room for added humiliation for the losers. Enter the Wheel of Water. The Wheel of Water is a free app that allows you to spin a wheel that gives you a method in which to douse the loser of the league (or a side bet) with water in ways that vary in style and humiliation. We made it for the pure joy of side bets and it is perfect for draft season when the weather is warm -- and even more rewarding in January when the weather is less forgiving. Putting something (ridiculous) on the line only adds to the enjoyment of your league. In fact, we have a yearly tradition that our league's loser has to endure one watering from every other league mate and then draft soaking wet. It's delightful.

COMMISSIONER'S CORNER

"What you stay focused on will grow." - Roy T. Bennett

◆ ◆ ◆

10. Get Your House In Order

If you're wondering when is the right time to make changes in your league, it is as Fatboy Slim so eloquently put, *"right here, right now."* Whether it's voting on rules, commissioner issues, draft day, deadline dates, or most importantly -- communication -- there has never been a better time to start the conversation than today. We all have busy lives, but constructing a few simple pillars for your league takes a small amount of concerted effort and pays off with a lifetime of fantasy football fun. Don't wait until the week before the draft to say "I really wish we had this" or "I wish I would've brought this up a month ago." Participants in your league need to know they are part of an ongoing conversation and part of a league that is always innovating. League members also want to be heard, so where you can involve them in majority or super-majority rule, do so.

11. Fix It!

If you've followed The Fantasy Footballers, you know that only one aspect of enjoying each and every fantasy football season is winning -- *"but if you're winning, you're grinning."* You should improve your league, make it fun, and realize that only 1 person wins in every league, but then the other 11 lose. You can take steps to make the **process** as fun as the **end result**:

- o Convert to a FAAB league?
- o League schedule adjustments?
- o No transaction restrictions
- o Eliminate old / uncommon / retired rules
- o Communication improvements
- o Reshuffle size (12 team league with 2 dead managers? Go to 10 man...etc)

12. Switch To Daily Waivers?

Traditional waivers run once a week -- usually on a Tuesday night or Wednesday morning depending on your league. However, the default setting in many leagues is that the rest of the week is open waivers. It's a first come, first serve basis. The problem is that if big news breaks such as an injury, the system rewards players who hear the news first and act immediately. Fantasy managers should not be punished for working jobs or spending time with their families. Continuous waivers run daily and allow for more interaction and bidding for free agents and the playing field is equal for everyone. In the end, you get to be part of a better league that anxiously waits for waivers every day. It's a recommendation we make for every league. The more strategy and touchpoints for daily check ins, the better.

13. No Vetoes!

Let me repeat: absolutely **NO vetoes**. 99% of the vetoed trades are canceled for petty reasons. "I don't want that team getting better" or "that manager isn't getting an equal value of that player" are not reasons to veto a trade. Leagues should enable instant trades with no processing or voting period. We all recognize that trading is one of the most enjoyable aspects of the game, so why are we limiting it with bogus vetoes? Everyone's player valuations are different, so let managers run their own team. The commissioner should only veto if collusion is obvious, and this is the only exception we make to the rule. Trust us -- this is better for everyone. You'd be surprised at how many trades look lopsided now, and are not the case later.

DRAFT DAY TRICKS

"You can't build a great building on a weak foundation." - Gordon B. Hinckley

◆ ◆ ◆

14. Live It Up At The Live Draft

Draft live and in person whenever possible! Make it an event that the league looks forward to all year. The winners get to gloat, you get to work trades in person, everyone gets to wear their favorite team gear, and you'll all enjoy some good old fashion trash talk and draft day grub. If you want people to take a league seriously, start with the draft. There's nothing like a draft room when you steal another manager's pick right before they make it, or when that one guy in the league drafts a player way, way too early. If you haven't experienced an in-person live draft, we strongly urge you to give it a try as a little pageantry goes a long way. Live drafting is a whole different level of drafting that, for some people, becomes an early Christmas present every year. If your league's live draft is important, make time and mark down days on your calendar to just think. Think about what this next year could look like or how you can make the draft experience as a league that much better. Upgrade draft day!

15. Know Your Surroundings

On draft day, whether you are in person or drafting on a computer, you need to know what the other teams are doing. Track whose other teams are drafting and mark it down. In a snake draft, knowing where other teams are in terms of filling roster positions like QBs or TEs allows you the freedom to not overreact and draft with confidence. Create a simple spreadsheet, or on a pen and paper mark which positions are taken by each manager. This is key in round-to-round decision making. At a minimum, the teams drafting right after or right before you should be carefully monitored, as it may allow you to skip a position and wait another round if your pick is not in jeopardy to be taken.

16. Tiering Up

Let us be clear. We cannot recommend a draft strategy more highly than "tier-based drafting." Having every single position in tiers breaks gives you a better picture of the gaps in draft value. This allows you to compare the eighth running back on your board and the fifth wide receiver on your board when you group players that are of similar value. A top-200 list is a useful overview but a tier-based drafting system helps you simply draft better. This strategy is extremely helpful when you're on the clock drafting and your sweating bullets, wondering *"Should I take a running back or a wide receiver?"* The Ultimate Draft Kit is focused on a tier-based drafting strategy.

17. No Risk It, No Biscuit

According to Jason, *"biscuits lead to diabetes."* What he's trying to communicate in his own unique way is choosing to avoid risk in the early rounds. Every year we assess each player with our own "risk rating" based on injury, situation, talent, and their range of outcomes. In the early rounds of a draft, mitigating risk is not about playing it safe, but rather playing it smart. Use your later picks to shoot for the moon and find a quarterback who could end up being a top-5 guy. Risk your biscuit in the 10th or 11th round on a tight-end rather than using up a high draft capital pick.

18. Not That Guy!

We all want to be objective and shrewd in how we draft our fantasy teams. However, sometimes we end up overthinking the process and end up with players on our teams we simply don't like. If you were a Bills fan (God bless you) and ended up taking a division rival's quarterback early, imagine the utter pain and self-harm you could cause yourself if the quarterback from the team you hate ends up costing you a fantasy victory. Don't do that to yourself. If you don't like the player or the team he plays, it's ok to pass. Remember this game is supposed to be fun, not cause a weekly hernia. It has to be a careful combination of technique and still enjoying the week-to-week.

COACHING
CONUNDRUMS

"Pressure is something you feel when you don't know what the hell you're doing." - Peyton Manning

◆ ◆ ◆

19. Reading The Tea Leaves

How do you sort out what a coach is saying in the offseason? In one moment, he's screaming for a committee approach in the backfield, and in the next breath he's comparing someone to Barry Sanders. During the offseason, much of the news and commentary from coaches can be described as hype and motivational. We can't always compute real numbers when a coach says his wide receiver can catch 100 passes in this offense. Beat writers are notorious for writing "puff pieces," exclaiming that certain players are in "the best shape of their career," or announcing that someone is running with the first team in practice. Slow down and read the tea leaves with caution. If there is any news to pay attention to, bad news is usually always bad news. It is rare, but when a coach does speak ill of a player or areas that are in need of improvement, take notice. We try to sort it out regularly for you on The Fantasy Footballers podcast.

20. Team Hype Can Be Tricky

The NFL is full of smart people. Defenses adjust year-to-year, so watch out for small sample sizes that spin into bigger narratives. Make note of the teams in the offseason that are gaining tons of hype that haven't actually shown it on the football field. Who could forget the "Dream Team Eagles" of 2011 with Michael Vick that finished 8-8. The Cleveland Browns of 2019 graced the cover of many magazines and media outlets en route to a 6-10 record and turned into an absolute train wreck. Be mindful when reading offseason situations. Everyone wants to project the next offensive powerhouse. That's the fun of fantasy, but realize that those "guaranteed" golden situations aren't always guaranteed. Things can and do go wrong, so when team hype elevates players to the point where they're no longer a fair or valuable draft day value, you might need to remember the Eagles or Browns of yesteryear. Everyone smells roses in the offseason, but the NFL field is a cruel reality for many narratives.

21. The Illusion Of Rational Coaching

Rational coaching assumes that the best players receive the most touches and the most playing time. Rational coaching would suggest the most talented players are on the field when you need them. On the contrary, these are human beings with a range of emotions, histories with organizations, and owners and coaching philosophies that are sometimes just downright irrational. We need to pause in assuming the best running back on the roster will be in there all three downs. Pull the reins on believing that the star rookie will see the majority of snaps right from the get-go. We all sit on our couches on a Sunday second-guessing every decision made by coaches. Build into your assumptions and draft strategies the fact that head coaches are not basing their decisions on fantasy football but on simply winning a game. At the end of the day, coaches prioritize many things beyond the fantasy stats you obsess over. This is unfortunate, but true. Accept the fact they're looking at different metrics than fantasy players for their decision making.

PARALYSIS BY ANALYSIS

"Cherish those who seek the truth but beware of those who find it." - Voltaire

◆ ◆ ◆

22. Year-End Fantasy Points Are Deceiving

We all love the final rankings and end-of-season numbers because they give us a numeric picture to gain closure. However, in fantasy, they don't give us a holistic picture of how that season actually played out. You have to figure out who actually helped your roster and who destroyed your week based on consistency metrics -- something we use every year. Often, players can gather a huge amount of production from just two to three *boom* weeks. Go back through the game logs and find out how many times a player "busted." Do not be deceived by the way it "feels" at the end of the year but look at whether they genuinely helped your roster week to week. Our consistency charts at TheFantasyFootballers.com are one of the key ways to identify players that actually performed.

23. Talent Can Win Out

Be mindful of the fact that talent and opportunity do not require a team to have a winning record. It's easy to let the stink of the team's record dissuade you. Discount bad teams at your own peril. Every year there are several players on teams with no visible hope, yet were consistent or dominant players. In the land of the modern NFL, players on losing teams can thrive week-in and week-out. Even with bad quarterbacks, even with losing teams, even with seemingly pathetic offenses or no hope as a franchise in the present, don't let defeat *defeat you*. In many ways, you have to look straight at opportunity with blinders on. In the modern NFL, catching up is a valuable part of a ballgame for fantasy managers.

24. Names Hurt (History And Hope)

What's in a name? Big names, historically productive names, and headline type of names all get stuck in the psyche of fantasy players and they don't let go. There have been several first round busts the last several years. Tears would stream down the face of the managers who believed in Eddie Lacy, C.J. Anderson, Jay Ajayi, Allen Robinson, and Jordy Nelson. The menacing nature of "history and hope" causes many players to be overdrafted. A lot of the time we want to believe a player's career isn't over, because we have seen them perform for fantasy players before. A name carries more weight than the reality of the situation. Be willing to let go of the past.

25. Know The End From The Beginning

Look at the players you like the most out of each round, especially when get to the later rounds. Our suggestion is to print out an ADP from the UDK and circle your favorites within each round. Step back and see what position(s) you actually like late in the draft. Maybe you're the reliable, value-based guy. Maybe you're the swing for the fences, home run hope type. After you're done, you might realize that you prefer late RB drafting or late WR drafting. That can inform the earlier part of your draft when you like both positions. There have been times in drafts where there are some late RBs/WRs that you absolutely want to walk away from the draft with. However, by the time you get to where they are going, your team dictates that you can't take them because you're in dire need for another position. Know the end, at least in part, from the beginning.

PLAYING LIKE A PRO

◆ ◆ ◆

26. Mock It Up

Now is the time to begin to get a "feel" for where players might be going before the rest of your league settles in. Mock drafting is like working out... except there is zero physical strain. Doing a couple of quick mock drafts allows you to work that drafting muscle and be able to notice which players are trending and moving. Try different strategies that you normally would be afraid to in a real draft. For instance, what would happen if you took a QB or TE early? Do you like the way your team plays out? Imagine you didn't get the RBs you wanted. How would you pivot? Grab your favorite drink and your drafting app and spend an afternoon poolside in the summer mock drafting away. It's no surprise the teams that succeed on draft day have been through a handful of mocks at a minimum.

27. Keep An Eye On The Ir

Know the rules of your league and platform where you play. Don't wait until a player gets injured to think about this spot. It's a free roster spot. Search out the players that have the "Out" or "IR" tag. This is a pre and a post draft maneuver that you can use to "gain" an extra shot at a player. If you catch it at the right time...you'll look like a genius and can activate that player down the line. Most leagues have spots, so take advantage.

28. Drop It Like It's Hot

Every time a waiver pickup happens, something else happens too. A player is dropped. Set your clocks. Put in those reminders on your phone. Make it a habit once a day to scour the waiver wire and find out who was dropped in your league when the waiver wire period took place the day before. Chances are many managers in your league weren't looking at anyone else's rosters when waivers went through but their own. There's nothing worse than when you go, "*NO! You got that guy!? How!?*" simply because you didn't notice he was dropped by a team completely unengaged. This is a quick way to gain an advantage by building it into your weekly fantasy football routine.

29. Memories Of Now

Don't underestimate the value of picking up a victory in the present versus building everything for future weeks. This is not to say you don't plan ahead while being wise, shrewd, and smart, but this week's matchup is before you. There are awesome ways to stay focused on this week's victory, such as trading a player that is about to go on bye for a player already through their bye. There is so much value in the present. Spend your FAAB early on players that have broken through. You'll be getting a difference maker that is right in front of your face versus the "theoretical" big signing based on an injury down the line. Sometimes, if you don't have a powerhouse squad, you need to buy weeks. It's not helpful to spend your waiver priority and FAAB bids in Week 10 if you're out of the playoffs. Consider the future but play for now. This becomes even easier as other teams "bow out" of title contention. Buy a week -- it's worth it, as nothing in the future is guaranteed. Maneuvering your way to weekly wins is key. Then maneuver again the following week.

30. Follow The Vegas Lines

If you're not paying attention to Vegas, now is the time to take notice that their bookmakers are extremely valuable in giving us an informed piece of the puzzle. Vegas moneymakers live and die by these numbers, so this isn't Joe-Somebody with an internet connection and a two-dollar website dishing out their opinion. When Vegas starts drawing totals upwards of 46, there are points to be scored in bunches. This seems to be the breaking point as you look specifically at favorites on teams with high projected totals. Don't try to predict game flow or guesstimate that the opposing team will continually be stopped at the 30-yard line on all their drives setting up field goals. Follow the lines, they'll serve you well for fantasy. The guys utilize the vegas lines in their weekly rankings.

I'M THINKING RB'S

"I feel like every running back should have their own little stamp on the game." - Arian Foster

◆ ◆ ◆

31. Buying The Two-For-One Special

Running backs are the most valuable commodity in fantasy football. There is such a clear competitive advantage especially in today's NFL when you consider the best fantasy running backs are also acting as elite WRs. Christian McCaffrey was essentially a top-12 RB on his rushing stats alone in the 2019 season and a top-15 WR on just his receiving stats. Together, he likely gave your team two-to-three players worth of points and an incredible weekly advantage. When you finish your draft, you should always skew towards having a few extra running backs on your bench. Running backs can gain much more value over time when injuries and opportunities pop up, while wide receivers can run about 40-50 deep.

32. Saddle A Stud

There are lots of ways to win at Fantasy Football. Some people argue for ZeroRB, or the "anti-fragile" theory of drafting. That CAN win... especially if you're in full PPR, 3 WR, multiple flex type leagues. But in the usual format that most of our leagues are playing in, it takes stud running backs at the core. You need a stud. You want a stud. You deserve a stud. And studs... are running backs. Depending on which data you're looking at, the most common position players on championship rosters are running backs. On average over the past two seasons, four of the top five players on championship teams are running backs. That makes sense because running backs are far more consistent. Securing a stud is key.

33. Prototypical Isn't Always The Best

Remember that prototypical isn't always best, even though it always feels best. In other words, when constructing a lineup, every single manager wants to be able to have stud running backs, top-end wide receivers, and the quarterback that basically breaks fantasy scoring. Remember this is a weekly game, so guys that aren't prototypical can still help carry your team. Allow for some out-of-the-box commitments from a slot wide receiver who might only get your 50 yards but rack up five or six catches. Be willing to take a chance on the quarterback with the subpar arm but makes it up with rushing production. If you can find a running back that pieces together ten touches from seven targets and three rushing attempts, maybe that's all you need to stabilize your roster that week.

34. Depth, Depth, Depth

Fantasy managers need to burn this word in their brain as it is the treasure trove you will need to pull from throughout the year to steady your sinking ship. On an annual basis, just under 25 percent of the top-50 picks are injured. Don't imagine you are going to come out unscathed. Don't give up, because injuries reconfigure the season and give opportunities where there didn't seem to be any. Any RB can become fantasy relevant at any part in the season due to injuries. Remember:

- **Draft for depth**
- **Play the waiver wire for depth**
- **Trade for depth**
- **Depth matters**

LET'S GET POSITIONAL

"You got one guy going boom, one guy going whack, and one guy not getting in the endzone." - John Madden

◆ ◆ ◆

35. Talking Qbs - Hold On To Your "Buts"

The quarterback position often is met with a few objections:

- **"But that QB stinks"**- With a perfect storm of home games and juicy matchups, you can depend on a streaming quarterback regardless of how good they are in real life. Long live Blake "the Snake" Bortles!
- **"But what about when that QB is playing poorly"** - An atrocious fantasy QB at the beginning of the season can easily turn it around given good matchups and enough time to return to the mean.
- **"But early QBs are safe!"**- Every year QBs are not only overdrafted but less than a quarter of them meet or exceed their draft position. There is often little capital gain from selecting a QB in Rounds 5-8 compared to waiting a bit longer. In other words, the difference of selecting the 6th or 7th QB off the board and the 12th or 13th is marginal in terms of end of season fantasy production. Quarterbacks drafted as QBs

9-17 routinely outperform their draft position by an average of five spots per year.
- **"But only elite QBs put up fantasy numbers!"**- Over 40 different QBs post top-12 weeks every year. Remember there are just 32 teams in the NFL…and how shocking that statistic is.

36. A History Of Rookies

There is a history of data that lends itself to approaching rookies:

- **Draft Rookie RBs** - Every year we have multiple rookie running backs that break into the league and assert themselves as a dominant fantasy force. Take a chance on a middle round guy competing in a supposed "backfield timeshare." Eventually, talent tends to win out.
- **Don't Draft Rookie WRs** - Outside of a couple outlier years, rookie WRs generally do not make a major fantasy impact right away. Some hit a rookie wall, while others occasionally shine in the second half after the coaching staff slowly gains trust and gives them the majority of snaps.
- **Don't Draft Rookie TEs** - Playing tight-end in the NFL is a major adjustment as most rookies spend half the year learning how to become a full-time blocker. It usually takes two or three years for a tight-end to pop up as a difference maker at the position in fantasy.
- **Draft Rookie Rushing QBs**- Cam Newton. Lamar Jackson. Kyler Murray. Take a chance on a QB with the mobility to become a game changer even as a rookie. There is a baseline of production that comes from running the ball that will hopefully make up for the mistakes but also give you the opportunity for monster upside in any given week.

37. Coupon Clipping Wide Receivers

It takes some time to pull out your scissors and clip those coupons before going to the grocery store. Yet the savings you receive is worth the investment of that menial task. If you want in on high average draft position players, see if there's a bargain wide receiver from that same team later on! The supposed WR2 on the team can end up with similar production with a drastically different draft opportunity cost than the proclaimed WR1. Take time to research the average draft position and make a list of five or so wide receivers who fit the mold of late value with some type of foreseeable upside if things break right this year. Sometimes finding the clearance item or diving into the bargain bin is exactly what you need. This happened years ago with tandems like Adam Thielen and Stefon Diggs. If both players have an opportunity, the coupon clipped part of the tandem is often the way to go.

38. Defense Matters... For The First Couple Of Weeks

Drafting defenses can often be out of sight and out of mind, but there is one simple research practice to perform each year in preparation for your draft. Look at the early season schedule when drafting fantasy defenses. Our Ultimate Draft Kit Strength of Schedule breaks down different time periods and uses more advanced metrics on a positional level than simply categorizing them as a "good team versus bad team." Home games against teams with young or volatile QBs often make for a perfect matchup, for example. Dig deeper for those matchup plays.

39. Ignore The Temptation Of Kicking

Kickers are easily the most frustrating part of playing fantasy. Many leagues, including our League of Record, have excommunicated them entirely from our rosters. If you are starting a kicker, don't be tempted to react from your previous year's misfortune and get cute by grabbing one early just because you had a Justin Tucker dream. Every year there is a large amount of unpredictability. Half of the top-12 kickers each year end up undrafted entirely. Streaming is still the best option at the position; look for high powered offenses or out-of-this-world legs. Stream it, boom-boom it, and *fuhgettaboutit*. Don't burn a high draft capital pick on a streamable position. Let someone else in your league think they are getting the advantage by drafting a kicker in the 10th round, and instead stream the position.

REMEMBER.
REMEMBER.
REMEMBER.

*"But the thing about remembering is that
you don't forget." - Tim O'Brien*

◆ ◆ ◆

40. Remember Your Trades

Remember the trades that failed, those that worked, and try to repeat the wins and avoid the mistakes. This might seem like common sense, but common sense can go a long way. For some, the process of tweaking an already great roster can also be the downfall of an impatient fantasy player. Whenever trading is on the table, every manager believes the grass is greener on the other side. This is a weekly game, but the context of fantasy football reveals that value and production changes quite frequently. We've seen many a roster get submarined by what seemed like polishing moves that undermined what the manager already had. Be smart and remember that depth is just as important as fine tuning a starting roster already on a roll.

41. Remember The Fallen

Guys coming back from injury are perennially underdrafted and doubted. Yes, their risk may be higher, but sometimes their bargain prices present upsides you don't want to forget. Value can be found in the forgotten fallen, especially if there is a good two or three round dip in what you think their perceived draft cost should be. Coming back from a major injury like an Achilles or ACL tear is gruesome, but some players' end of season stats are simply stunted due to outlier or freak injury that caused them to miss only a handful of games. Don't forget how good a season can be wrecked by injuries that drive down the average draft position to your benefit. Other fantasy players tend to favor the player with recent success, not the bounce back player.

42. Remember: The Power Of The Scat-Back

The cornerstone of any successful fantasy team in the early 2000s was the 300+ carry running back. We always want to take the player that can turn into an Adrian Peterson workhorse. Unfortunately, every running back doesn't have the chance to be the bell-cow. However, if you only view fantasy football with that approach, you might miss out on highly consistent and valuable pieces. RB targets are worth almost double the fantasy points as a rushing attempt. This means a player seeing 60 targets and 100 rushing attempts on the season can be worth as much as a 200+ carry starter. Once a guy is an established pass-catcher, he tends to be utilized that way for...just about forever, especially if he remains in the same system. You can lean on these running backs to carry you through weeks despite them not appearing to be heavy workload options. Take a chance in the draft and one of them might hit. More importantly, don't be put off by the reality that some running backs are essentially wide receivers.

43. Remember: The Power Of The Streaming Quarterback

Signing a QB off the waiver wire and starting them that week takes some serious courage in fantasy football. Every week, we have a segment on our podcast where we select three streaming options off the waiver. Over the last several years, the average result from this strategy was the QB6. As you move deeper into the fantasy season, it becomes more difficult to display the mental fortitude needed to pivot off of a star QB and stream someone else who might be inferior in the NFL but has a plus matchup for fantasy. Even peak Aaron Rodgers or Peyton Manning have lost people fantasy championships; Blake Bortles has won fantasy championships. Selecting a QB late in drafts allows you to be able to adjust on the fly if your starter isn't living up to your expectations. Streaming the quarterback position in single quarterback leagues is often essential for roster depth unless you managed to hit on a superstar in the later rounds.

44. Remember, Age Is Just A Number

Time and time again age is overvalued in the dynasty realm. Remember, age is simply a number that does not necessarily define a player's output in the NFL. As a rule of thumb, WRs tend to offer longer shelf lives than RBs in terms of career paths. As a result, experienced dynasty managers usually assemble a roster around a young core of receivers. The same logic does not have to apply to the remaining pieces of a team, as a blend of veteran and ascending talent typically result in annual success. Those who build a team for the future often find it difficult to compete if prospects fail to pan out. Identify players with a year or two of top production left and you may find them to be cheaper in dynasty leagues yet lead you to championships.

TRADE LIKE A CHAMPION

"There is nothing more deceptive than an obvious fact." - Arthur Conan Doyle

◆ ◆ ◆

45. Master Of Trades

Exact value in a trade is not an exact science. If you are getting the best overall player in a trade, it's often ok to overpay. *A two-for-one trade is not a two-for-one deal*; it includes the player you are receiving AND a player that you will end up able to pick up on waivers! Everyone in the league looks at their own players through rose-colored glasses. Sometimes it's best to send some shock-and-awe deals. You need to understand how a manager views and is using a specific player. One of the worst trades comes from the manager who doesn't recognize the value to your roster construction. Unless you like getting your offers immediately declined, don't send an offer that would result in the other manager losing a starter for a bench player. Meet someone else's needs -- or manipulate them into thinking you are -- and you have a better shot.

46. Don't Spam Offers

Everyone hates spam, and we don't mean that processed meat in a can. We're talking the junk you get in your email, in your mailbox, or on your phone. There is so much spam everywhere we turn, we don't need it creeping into our fantasy football leagues. Don't be that manager that blindly shoots out a trade offer to every single team in the league. No one believes that your rich uncle is really trying to help their fantasy team. It's perfectly fine to toss out a few offers to managers you know, but if you want the whole league to know that you're shopping a player, use the league management programs trade bait area. Bad offers can turn into a boy who cried wolf situation that leads to none of your offers being taken seriously.

47. Respond To Trade Offers

"You catch more flies with honey than
you do with vinegar." -Andy

Have a little common courtesy and respond to trade offers. Even if it means immediately declining it, do something. Nothing is worse than sending a trade offer and having the other manager acting like it never happened. This is also why it's so important to have an open dialogue outside the league hosting site. Andy likes to approach trades with the concept that any player is available. It's all about price.

48. Opportunistic Dynasty Trading

If you're wondering when it's the right time to open up conversation for trading in a dynasty league, that moment is right now. Trading players before certain benchmarks in the NFL calendar is so crucial. Before the NFL Draft, after the NFL Draft, and during training camp are all vital moments to take advantage of. You want to trade a player with his full potential built into the value of the trade; it doesn't even matter if it pans out. For example, if someone thinks a player is an RB1 and is willing to pay that price, jump on an opportunity. Overvaluing the unknown for the known leads to being stagnant. Have a balance on each team and cash-in for some lottery tickets.

THE DO NOTS

"Trees that are slow to grow bear the best fruit." - Moliere

◆ ◆ ◆

49. Do Not Bail... Ever.

"Whatever happens, can happen in reverse." - Andy

You need to stay active ALL season. We've heard countless stories of fantasy managers starting 0-3, 0-4, or even 0-5 and coming back to make the playoffs and win the championship. The integrity of the entire league is disrupted as soon as even a single manager starts to bail. Be an active manager for yourself and for your league mates. Mike has said that if he's already out of playoff contention near the end of the season, he's angry and not letting up. He's not going to take it easy on the waiver wire, he's not giving an opponent an easy win -- he's going to wreak havoc! What's great about staying connected is that you may have others in the league who don't, creating a much easier pathway to entering playoff contention. That 0-4 start can turn into a 4-0 run and put you right back in the thick of things.

50. Do Not Play Afraid- Part 1

Mike is known for quoting Ice Cube - *"If you're scared, go to church"* - you can't play scared! Scared players do scared things. Scared players draft useless backups as insurance. Stop using a roster spot on a meaningless backup that is dependent on your starter being hurt to have any value or upside. Sometimes, it's better with a flier you can actually flip in trades or see develop into a standalone value. Scared players won't draft multiple players with matching bye weeks. Yet by the time the bye weeks actually come, in most leagues, your roster has turned over via trade and waivers. Don't let such things cloud your vision. Don't play scared, play aggressively and be willing to adapt. You have to play to *win,* not play to not lose.

51. Do Not Play Afraid- Part 2

Scared players must fill their starting roster before their bench in drafts. If you adopt this strategy, you will end up drafting a QB or TE too early. You'll miss out on many of the positions in which depth is crucial, and where you start multiple players of the same position. Scared players are always looking over their shoulder for validation. Scared players rethink their draft strategy because a mock draft tool gives them a bad grade. STOP playing scared.

52. Do Not Overreact To Week 1!

Deep Breaths... now that you have inundated your brain with information, take a deep breath and don't tilt when your team doesn't perform the way you hoped. Stay calm and don't sell a player you were over the moon about on draft day at 25% of his value after Week 1. Don't overpay when an unheralded player goes for 45 fantasy points in Week 1. If you look at the season as a whole, outlier performances happen every single week. But when it's Week 1, it becomes magnified. It's ripe for confirmation bias. A single week's performance can be taken as proof of the truth. It's not. Due to the mental investment of an offseason of research, it can be easy to jump ship. However, on the flip side, if someone else is hyperventilating after Week 1, jump right in. Stay above the overreactions.

53. Do Not Get Sentimental About Players (Love Hurts)

Fantasy players can build an idyllic starting roster often at the expense of draft capital, and then gawk at it, post it on their mirror, and write in their diary about it's many wonderful qualities. They fall in love. Sometimes you have to be willing to make another diary entry and be able to pivot and move on. You could feel stuck starting this guy no matter what. It's the classic "sunk cost" fallacy. Because you've invested so much, pivoting off starting this player becomes that much more difficult. We all fall in love especially in dynasty and keeper leagues! You can't win on paper. You don't get to count last year's points this year. You don't get bonus points if you own the players jersey. You don't get a head start this year by holding on to last year. Try your best to be objective, view each season as a fresh one, and start anew. Don't be sentimental.

54. Do Not Smell Your Own Farts

Sometimes your team just isn't that good... Jason often uses the phrase "*smelling your own farts*" in terms of enjoying the stink that your fantasy football team is creating. You have "your guys." This can cause us to have biased views of our team. Many managers think all their players are the best, no one else's are good, and turn down advantageous trades because of that bias. You have to call a spade a spade, and a fart a fart. It doesn't do you any good pretending to still be in love with a fart. The solution is having more players waiting in the wings and leaning on depth when your star players aren't coming through the way you want. Be willing to adjust your expectations when reality doesn't match your prognostication, the experts hopes and dreams, or what you envisioned them doing.

A FINAL NOTE

◆ ◆ ◆

55. You Get What You Give

Fantasy football amplifies everything we love about the NFL. As with anything in life, when it comes to playing in a fantasy football league, you get what you give. Everything we do at The Fantasy Footballers is about making your season more enjoyable. If you're a commissioner, your league often goes just as you go. What you put in as a commish is what you get out. Little things and little traditions go a long way. Loser punishments, draft rituals, weekly power rankings written up by leaguemates, trading blocks, centralized Slack channels or Facebook groups, etc. Every little addition builds your league from being a ho-hum league into a powerhouse league. The kind of league you have a waiting list to get into. You get what you give, and we encourage you to give a lot and build your league and team into the best it can be. We'll help.

ACKNOWLEDGEMENT

"There is little success where there is little laughter." - Andrew Carnegie

Special thanks to our editor-in-chief and Fantasy Footballers DFS Podcast host Kyle Borgognoni, who tirelessly collected and distilled insights from our many episodes over the years for use in this book.

To our staff and all those involved with the production and distribution of The Fantasy Footballers Podcast, thank you for all you do. You make every day a joy to come to work.

ABOUT THE AUTHOR

The Fantasy Footballers

The Fantasy Footballers podcast is an award-winning independent fantasy football podcast that records and produces fantasy football content all year long. The show is focused on producing and developing content that is highly accurate, highly entertaining, and of a high production quality.

The show debuted in 2014 and is hosted by Andy Holloway, Jason Moore, and Mike "The Fantasy Hitman" Wright. As three longtime friends and former tech/gaming professionals, they saw a need for a fresh take in the fantasy football universe, so they hiked up their trousers, combed their beards, and went to work.

The Fantasy Footballers make it a priority to focus on a holistic approach to fantasy football expertise and advice. Fantasy football is more than stat sheets and excel docs. It's about strategy, it's about league formation and communication, it's about trading strategies and draft day. It's about winning the mental game, reading between the lines, finding the diamonds in the rough, and mocking your friends while you succeed.

The podcast itself is distributed across a wide range of podcast distributors, including but not limited to Apple Podcasts, Google Podcasts, Spotify, Stitcher, and anywhere else you listen to podcasts. It can also be watched on YouTube.

The die hard fans of The Fantasy Footballers are affectionately called the #FootClan, a tight knit fantasy community that can be found at JoinTheFoot.com. As a completely independent podcast without network backing, the show exists in part based on the support of the community as well as show advertisers. To learn more about supporting the show, visit JoinTheFoot.com.

Made in the USA
Coppell, TX
26 July 2022

80449303R00031